THE POWER OF DAILY PLEASURES

HOW TO BRING MORE JOY AND HAPPINESS INTO YOUR LIFE

BY: HICHAM BEN

DISCLAIMER

The information provided in this book is intended for general informational and educational purposes only. It is not intended to be a substitute for professional advice, diagnosis, or treatment. Always seek the advice of a qualified healthcare provider with any questions you may have regarding a medical condition.
The information in this book is based on the author's research and personal experiences and is not intended to be a substitute for professional advice.
The author cannot be held responsible for any damage or injury that may result from the use of the information provided in this book.
The author has made every effort to ensure the accuracy of the information in this book but does not guarantee that it is free from errors or omissions.
The author does not accept any liability for any inaccuracies or errors in this book.

Please note that the information in this book may be subject to change without notice and the author does not undertake to update this book.

This disclaimer applies to the entire content of this book and any related materials. By purchasing and reading this book, you accept and agree to be bound by the terms of this disclaimer.

Published by [HICHAM BEN]

ISBN: 9798374540130

[https://kdp.amazon.com]

TABLE OF CONTENTS

TABLE OF

CONTENTS

TABLE OF
CONTENTS

TABLE OF

CONTENTS

TABLE OF
CONTENTS

Introduction

In today's fast-paced world, it's easy to get caught up in the hustle and bustle of daily life and forget to take the time to enjoy the simple things.

We often focus on our responsibilities and obligations, neglecting the importance of pleasure in our lives. However, incorporating daily pleasures into our lives can have a significant impact on our overall well-being.

This book is designed to help readers understand the concept of daily pleasures and how to incorporate them into their daily lives.

Through a combination of practical advice, strategies, and real-life examples, readers will learn how to find and make time for daily pleasures, overcome obstacles that keep them from experiencing pleasure and build a supportive community around daily pleasures.

The book will also explore the intersection of daily pleasures and self-care, and the impact of self-care on overall daily pleasures in life.

The Power of Daily Pleasures *is a guide to a new way of thinking about the importance of pleasure in our lives. It will change the way you think about pleasure and show you how to make it a priority in your daily life.*

It will provide readers with practical advice and strategies for incorporating daily pleasures into their lives, as well as inspiration for finding daily pleasures in everyday moments.

CHAPTER I

Understanding the Concept of Daily Pleasures

In this chapter, we will explore the concept of daily pleasures and the role they play in our lives. We will define what daily pleasures are and the benefits of incorporating them into our daily lives.

First, let's define what we mean by daily pleasures. Daily pleasures are small, everyday activities or experiences that bring us joy, happiness, and contentment. They can be simple things like taking a walk in nature, having a cup of tea, or reading a book. They can also be more complex activities like playing an instrument, taking a yoga class, or spending time with loved ones.

Daily pleasures are the small things that make life worth living, they are the things that bring us a sense of joy and happiness in our everyday lives. They are not the same as big, life-changing events like getting a promotion or buying a new car.

Now, let's talk about the benefits of incorporating daily pleasures into our lives. Daily pleasures can have a significant impact on our overall well-being. They can:

- *Increase our sense of happiness and contentment: Taking the time to engage in activities that bring us joy and pleasure can improve our mood, reduce stress and anxiety and increase our overall sense of well-being.*
- *Improve our physical and mental health: Engaging in pleasurable activities can also have a positive impact on our physical and mental health. For example, physical activities like yoga, dancing, or gardening can improve our physical fitness, and mental activities such as reading, painting, or listening to music can improve*

our mental health.

- *Enhance our relationships with others: Incorporating daily pleasures into our lives can also have a positive impact on our relationships with others. For example,*
- *spending quality time with loved ones, going on a date with your partner, or having a picnic with friends can strengthen our relationships and bring us closer together.*
- *Increase our overall satisfaction with life: Engaging in daily pleasures can also increase our overall satisfaction with life. When we take the time to enjoy the small things in life, we can appreciate what we have and be more content with our lives.*

Incorporating daily pleasures into our lives can also have a positive impact on our productivity and motivation. When we take the time to enjoy daily pleasures, we are better able to handle the challenges of daily life. It can help us to stay focused and motivated, and to achieve our goals and aspirations.

In this chapter, we have discussed the concept of daily pleasures and the benefits of incorporating them into our lives. We have also discussed the importance of identifying and prioritizing our daily pleasures and creating a plan to incorporate them into our daily lives. In the next chapter, we will explore strategies for incorporating daily pleasures into our daily routine and practical tips for finding daily pleasures in everyday activities.

CHAPTER II

Identifying and Prioritizing Your Daily Pleasures

In this chapter, we will focus on how to identify and prioritize your daily pleasures. Understanding what brings you joy and fulfillment is an important step in incorporating daily pleasures into your life.

The first step in identifying and prioritizing your daily pleasures is to assess your current daily pleasure patterns. This includes taking a look at the activities you currently engage in that bring you joy and fulfillment. It's important to consider both the activities you engage in regularly and those that you occasionally indulge in.

This will give you a clear picture of your current pleasure patterns and help you identify areas where you can incorporate more daily pleasures into your life.

The next step is to set goals for incorporating more daily pleasures into your life. This can be done by setting specific, measurable, and achievable goals that are tailored to your unique interests and needs. For example, if you enjoy reading, your goal might be to read a book every week. If you enjoy cooking, your goal might be to try a new recipe every month. Setting goals helps you to stay focused and motivated, and it also allows you to measure your progress over time.

Creating a daily pleasure plan is the final step in identifying and prioritizing your daily pleasures. This plan should include specific activities that you want to incorporate into your daily routine and a schedule for when you will engage in these activities.

It's important to schedule your daily pleasures in advance to ensure that you make time for them. This will help you to stay on track and make sure that you are incorporating daily pleasures into your life on a regular basis.

In this chapter, we have discussed the importance of identifying and prioritizing your daily pleasures, and provided strategies for assessing your current daily pleasure patterns, setting goals for incorporating more daily pleasures into your life, and creating a daily pleasure plan. By following these steps, readers will be able to understand their unique pleasure patterns and create a plan to incorporate more daily pleasures into their lives.

A Quote

"Life is a journey, daily pleasures are the moments of joy that make it worth taking"

CHAPTER III

Incorporating Daily Pleasures into Your Daily Routine

In this chapter, we will focus on how to incorporate daily pleasures into your daily routine. We will provide tips and strategies for finding daily pleasures in everyday activities, as well as examples of daily pleasure-enhancing activities

.

One of the keys to incorporating daily pleasures into your daily routine is to be mindful of the activities that you engage in on a daily basis. Many of these activities offer opportunities for incorporating daily pleasures if we take the time to look for them.

For example, taking a walk in nature, listening to music while doing household chores, or enjoying a cup of tea during a break at work.

Another strategy for incorporating daily pleasures into your daily routine is to make a conscious effort to include them in your work and home life. This can be done by setting aside a specific time for daily pleasures during the workday, such as taking a short break to read a book or listen to music. At home, you can incorporate daily pleasures into your daily routine by setting aside time for hobbies or activities that you enjoy, such as cooking, gardening, or crafting.

We will also provide specific examples of daily pleasure-enhancing activities that can be incorporated into your daily routine. For example, practicing mindfulness or meditation, engaging in physical activities like yoga or dance, or listening to an uplifting podcast while commuting to work. All of these activities can bring joy and fulfillment to your daily routine.

It's also important to be open to new experiences and try new things. This can help to expand your pleasure patterns and discover new activities that bring you joy.

In this chapter, we have discussed strategies for incorporating daily pleasures into your daily routine and provided practical tips for finding daily pleasures in everyday activities. We have also emphasized the importance of being mindful of the small things in life that bring you pleasure, and being open to new experiences and trying new things.

A Quote

"Life is too short to not make time for the little things that bring us joy"

CHAPTER IV

Overcoming Obstacles to Daily Pleasures

This chapter focuses on the common obstacles that people face when trying to incorporate daily pleasures into their lives. It covers the internal barriers such as guilt and shame, and the external obstacles that can make it difficult to engage in daily pleasures

One of the most common obstacles to incorporating daily pleasures into our lives is guilt. Many people feel guilty for taking time for themselves, or for engaging in activities that they enjoy.

They may feel that they should be focusing on more important or productive things, or that they don't deserve to engage in pleasurable activities.
Shame is another common obstacle, many people feel ashamed of the things that bring them pleasure. They may feel that their interests or hobbies are not socially acceptable, or that they are not good enough to engage in pleasurable activities.

The chapter also provides strategies for overcoming these internal barriers such as recognizing that it is normal to have these feelings and that it's important to practice self-compassion and self-care. Additionally, the chapter provides tips for addressing external obstacles such as lack of time or financial resources. For example, finding free or low-cost alternatives to expensive activities, or finding ways to make time for daily pleasures within a busy schedule.

In this chapter, we have explored the intersection of daily pleasures and self-care, and the impact of self-care on overall daily pleasure in life. We have discussed how incorporating daily pleasures into our lives can be a form of self-care and how taking care of ourselves can also help us to find and make time for daily pleasures. We also emphasized the importance of being mindful of the impact of self-care on overall daily pleasure in life.

A Quote

"Self-care and daily pleasures go hand in hand, one cannot be truly fulfilled without the other"

CHAPTER V

The Intersection of Daily Pleasures and Self-Care

In this chapter, we will delve deeper into the connection between daily pleasures and self-care and examine the impact of self-care on our overall daily pleasure in life.

Self-care is the practice of taking care of oneself, both physically and mentally. It's the act of taking time to nurture and care for oneself, and it's an important aspect of overall well-being. Daily pleasures and self-care are closely related. Incorporating daily pleasures into our lives can be a form of self-care, and taking care of ourselves can also help us to find and make time for daily pleasures.

For example, engaging in physical activities such as yoga or dancing can be both a daily pleasure and a form of self-care. These activities can help to improve our physical fitness and reduce stress. Similarly, engaging in mental activities such as reading, painting, or listening to music can be both a daily pleasure and a form of self-care. These activities can help to improve our mental health and reduce stress.

It's also important to understand the impact of self-care on overall daily pleasure in life. When we take care of ourselves, we are better able to handle the challenges of daily life. This can help us to stay focused, and motivated and achieve our goals and aspirations. Furthermore, self-care can help us to be more resilient and to cope better with stress and difficult situations. This can help us to be more content with our lives and to appreciate the small things that bring us pleasure.

In this chapter, we will discuss how to integrate daily pleasure and self-care practices, for example, how the practice of gratitude can enhance both daily pleasure and self-care, or how engaging in mindfulness activities can bring benefits to both.

We will also touch upon the importance of balancing self-care with self-compassion, and the impact of self-compassion on daily pleasure and overall well-being.

We will also examine how addressing the barriers to self-care, such as lack of time, energy, or resources, can also improve our ability to incorporate daily pleasures into our lives.

Overall, this chapter aims to highlight the close relationship between daily pleasures and self-care and to provide practical strategies for integrating them in order to enhance overall well-being.

A Quote

" Daily pleasures are the secret ingredient to a fulfilling and happy life "

CHAPTER VI

Building a Supportive Community

In this chapter, we will delve deeper into the importance of building a supportive community around daily pleasures and provide more specific strategies for finding and connecting with individuals who share your interests. Having a community of individuals who share your passion for daily pleasures can be incredibly beneficial for our overall well-being. Not *only does it provide motivation and accountability, but it also fosters a sense of belonging and connection, which is essential for our mental and emotional health.*

One way to find like-minded individuals is to connect through online communities, social media groups, or local clubs and organizations. These communities can offer support, inspiration, and opportunities for shared activities and experiences. It's a great way to connect with people who have similar interests and to learn from each other. It can also be a great source of inspiration and motivation.

Another approach is to engage in shared activities with friends and family. For example, if you enjoy gardening, you can plan a gardening day with your friends or family. If you enjoy cooking, you can plan a cooking class with your loved ones. Sharing your passion with others can be a great way to build stronger relationships and create lasting memories.

Additionally, it is important to be open to new experiences and try new things. This can help to expand your pleasure patterns and discover new activities that bring you joy. It can also lead to new connections and friendships. Being open to new experiences can also help you to see things from a different perspective and can bring a sense of excitement and adventure to your life.

Furthermore, it's important to take advantage of local resources and events to find like-minded individuals. For example, attending local events such as art shows, music festivals, or food fairs can be a great way to meet new people who share your interests. Joining a local sports team, club or organization can also be a great way to meet new people and build connections.

Also, it's crucial to be mindful and respectful of other people's boundaries when building a community. It's important to respect each other's preferences and to be open to different perspectives and opinions

A Quote

"Pleasure is not a luxury, it's a necessary component of well-being"

VII - Conclusion

THE POWER OF DAILY PLEASURES IN OUR LIVES

In this book, we have explored the concept of daily pleasures, the role they play in our overall well-being, and strategies for incorporating them into our daily lives. We have discussed the importance of identifying and prioritizing our daily pleasures, incorporating them into our daily routines, overcoming obstacles, and building a supportive community. We have also examined the intersection of daily pleasures and self-care, and the impact of self-care on overall daily pleasures in life.

The potential of incorporating daily pleasures into our daily lives is enormous. Daily pleasures have the power to enhance our overall well-being by improving our physical and mental health, reducing stress, and increasing our sense of happiness and contentment. By incorporating daily pleasures into our daily lives, we can improve our overall quality of life, and find more meaning and purpose in our daily activities.

It's important to note that incorporating daily pleasures into our lives is a continuous process, and it's important to continue to prioritize them. Daily pleasures should be incorporated into our daily routines, and it's important to make time for them every day. This can be achieved by setting specific goals and creating a daily pleasure plan, and by being open to new experiences.

In conclusion, the role of daily pleasures in overall well-being is crucial.

They have the power to improve our physical and mental health, reduce stress, and increase our sense of happiness and contentment. Incorporating daily pleasures into our daily lives can improve our overall quality of life and provide a sense of meaning and purpose.

It's important to continue to prioritize daily pleasures and to make time for them every day. It's also important to build a supportive community around daily pleasures and to be open to new experiences and perspectives.

A Quote

"Daily pleasures are the secret ingredient to a fulfilling and happy life"

VIII - The End

As you come to the end of this book, we want to express our gratitude for taking the time to read it. We hope that you have found the information and strategies presented in this book to be valuable and that you have been able to apply them to your own life.

Incorporating daily pleasures into your life has the power to enhance your overall well-being and improve the quality of your life. We hope that this book has provided you with the tools and knowledge you need to make this happen.

We encourage you to continue to prioritize daily pleasures in your life, to set goals and make a plan to incorporate them into your daily routine and to share your daily pleasures with others.

Remember, incorporating daily pleasures into your life is an ongoing process and it's important to continue to make it a priority.

Thank you again for reading this book. We wish you all the best in your journey to incorporate daily pleasures into your life and improve your overall well-being.

Thank you

The key to a happy life is finding pleasure in the everyday

www.ingramcontent.com/pod-product-compliance
Lightning Source LLC
LaVergne TN
LVHW020528160826
845677LV00015B/3963
9798374540130